Usbor

C

Anna Milbourne

Designed by Michelle Lawrence

Illustrated by Patrizia Donaera and Christyan Fox

Cat consultant: Claire Bessant

Reading consultant: Alison Kelly
University of Surrey Roehampton

SCHOLASTIC INC.
New York Toronto London Auckland Sydney
Mexico City New Delhi Hong Kong Buenos Aires

Contents

A new family

A mother cat finds a warm, safe place to have her kittens.

The kittens are born. One by one, the mother cat licks them clean.

Growing up

New kittens cuddle up to their mother to keep warm.

They sleep most of the time.

A mother cat has six teats on her tummy. Her kittens suck them to drink her milk.

Kittens are born with their eyes shut. After about ten days, they open their eyes.

About two weeks later, they learn to walk. This kitten is taking its first steps.

They grow teeth and start to eat meat. Soon, they stop drinking milk.

All kittens have blue eyes to begin with.
Later, they can turn green or yellow or orange.

Playing

Kittens like to play. They learn how to do things by playing games.

These kittens are play-fighting.

They won't really hurt each other.

Grown-up pet cats like to play, too. It stops them from getting bored.

Kittens pretend to hunt. A kitten creeps up to its mother's tail.

It pounces and catches the tail with its paws.

Some kittens live in the wild, like this lynx. It likes to play too, but it will have to hunt and fight for real when it grows up.

Leaving home

To make good pets, kittens have to get used to people before they are eight weeks old.

Kittens learn to be friendly by copying their mother.

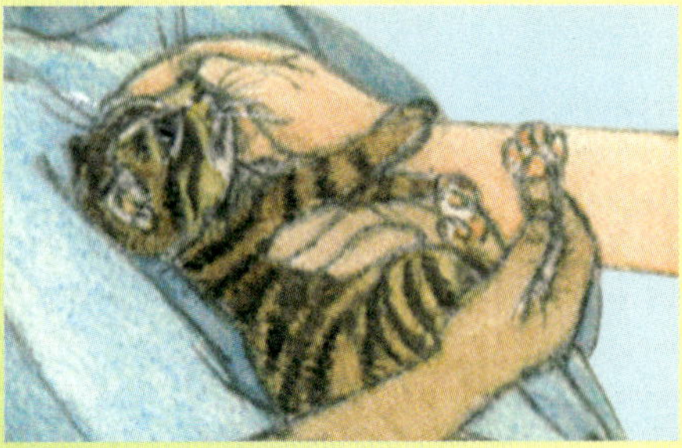

If they meet lots of friendly people, they learn to like people.

When a kitten is about eight weeks old, it is ready to leave its mother.

Cats that grow up without getting used to people are shy.

These cats are feral. This means they are half wild. Lots of feral cats live in cities. They live in little groups and take care of themselves.

Pet cats normally live for about 12 to 14 years. The longest a pet cat has ever lived is 34 years.

Cat talk

You can tell how a cat feels by the way it looks and acts.

If a cat rolls onto its back, then it feels safe with you.

Cats stare at each other if they want to fight. If you blink at a cat, you can make it feel safe.

If a cat wags its tail, leave it alone. It may be feeling angry.

If a cat partly closes its eyes and purrs, it means it feels happy.

If a cat looks at you and says "meow", it wants something.

A cat in danger curves its back to look bigger and scare off its enemy.

Climbing

Cats like to jump and climb. They feel safe in high places.

They have sharp claws that help them hold on as they climb.

If a cat falls, it tries to land on its feet, so it doesn't hurt itself.

As it falls, the cat twists its head and front legs around.

Then, the cat twists its back legs around.

The cat curves its back. This helps it land softly.

Hunting

Cats are good hunters.

This pet cat is jumping to try to catch a bird.

Pet cats are fed at home, so they don't need to hunt for food.

A cat can jump about five times its own height. How high can you jump?

Wild cats have to hunt for their food.

A hungry wild cat hears a mouse. It crouches down to hide in the grass.

It creeps slowly toward the mouse. The cat's furry paws help it walk very quietly.

When it is close to the mouse, the cat pounces and catches it.

Smells

Cats can smell smells that people can't. They know who other cats are by their smell.

When cats say hello, they sniff each other.

They rub their bodies together to share their smells.

Pet cats rub up against people to say hello, too.

Pet cats scratch things in their owner's house to show it's their home, too.

Cats mark their home area with their smells, so that other cats know it is theirs.

This kitten is rubbing its head on a tree to leave its smell there.

Cross cats

Some cats don't like others being near their home. This is how a cat warns another off.

A black cat comes near an orange cat's home. The orange cat stares hard at it.

The black cat crouches and looks away. This shows it doesn't want to fight.

The black cat creeps away again. The orange cat has won.

Cats hiss, growl and scream when they fight.

Cats don't like fighting. But if they can't warn an enemy off by staring, they might fight.

A cat hisses and then it tries to scratch its enemy with its claws.

Nightlife

Cats like to go out in the evening. They can see in the dark better than people can.

In bright light, a cat's pupils look like slits.

In dim light, a cat's pupils grow big. This lets in any light that's there, so it can see.

A cat's eyes glow if light shines on them when it's dark.

When it's too dark to see, a cat's long whiskers help it feel its way around.

The tips of the cat's whiskers touch the edges of a fence.

The cat knows it can fit through the fence, so it walks through.

Catnap

Cats look for warm, quiet places to sleep.

If it's hot they sleep stretched out.

If it's a little cooler they sleep curled up.

Cats like to sleep. They have lots of quick naps through the day.

This kitten has climbed a tree for a nap.

This cat has just woken up and is stretching. Stretching helps a cat to wake up and get ready for action.

A cat spends over half of its life asleep.

Keeping clean

Cats wash themselves to keep clean. Follow the numbers to see how a cat washes itself.

1. The cat licks its paw. It wipes the wet paw on its face.

2. It nibbles its paws to clean dirt off and to tidy its claws.

3. It nibbles at any knots in its fur to get them out.

4. It licks its legs, its whole body and then its tail.

Sometimes cats help to lick each other clean.
This shows they are good friends.

A cat's tongue is very rough. When a cat licks its fur, its tongue works like a comb.

Fur

Cats' fur helps keep them warm. Some cats have short fur and some have long, bushy fur.

This kind of cat is called a Persian cat. They have very long fur.

In summer, some of a cat's fur falls out, so the cat doesn't get too hot. This is called shedding.

Cats can have different patterns on their fur. Even kittens in the same family can all look different.

Siamese cats have dark ears, faces, tails and paws. They aren't born this way.

The kittens are born pale cream all over.

Later, some parts of their bodies turn dark.

Kinds of cats

There are lots of unusual kinds of pet cats. Different kinds of cats are called breeds.

Here are some examples of cat breeds.

Munchkin cats have short legs.

Siamese cats are slim.

Sphynxes have hardly any fur.

This cat is a Turkish Van. Most cats hate water, but Turkish Vans love swimming.

Manx cats have no tails.

Norwegian Forest cats have long, bushy tails.

Most pet cats are a mixture of breeds.

Glossary of cat words

Here are some of the words in this book you might not know. This page tells you what they mean.

teat - a mother cat has teats on her tummy. Kittens drink milk from them.

feral - a half-wild animal. Lots of feral cats live in cities or on farms.

claw - sharp parts on a cat's paws. Claws are an animal's fingernails.

hunt - to find, chase and kill another animal, usually to eat.

pupil - the black part in the middle of an animal's or a person's eye.

nap - a short sleep. Cats nap often, so sometimes naps are called catnaps.

shedding - losing fur. Cats shed in the summer to keep cool.

Websites to visit

If you have a computer, you can find out more about cats on the Internet. On the Usborne Quicklinks website there are links to four fun websites.

Website 1 - Play a cat game.

Website 2 - Learn more about pet cats and how to take care of them.

Website 3 - Draw a cartoon cat.

Website 4 - Find out about wild cats.

To visit these websites, go to **www.usbornequicklinks.com** and type the keywords "beginners cats". Then click on the link for the website you want to visit. Before you use the Internet, look at the safety guidelines inside the back cover of this book and ask an adult to read them with you.

Index

Acknowledgements

Managing editor: Fiona Watt
Managing designer: Mary Cartwright
Photographic manipulation by Emma Julings

Photo credits

The publishers are grateful to the following for permission to reproduce material: © **Alamy Images:** 6; © **Ardea London:** 4 (François Gohier), 19 (Pat Morris); © **Corbis:** title (Pat Doyle), 9 (James Marshall), 27 (Julie Habel); © **Getty:** cover (Gary Randall), 12 (Sue Streeter), 21(Desmond Burdon), 26 (Barros & Barros); © **Graeme Teague:** 25; © **ImageState:** 8 (Robert Llewellyn), 22 (Leland Howard), 23 (Veturian); © **Photonica:** 10 (Neo Vision); © **Team Husar:** 7 (Lisa & Mike Husar); © **Warren Photographic:** 14; 3, 17, 20, 28 (Jane Burton); 31 (Jane Burton)

 First published in Great Britain in 2003 by Usborne Publishing Ltd.

ISBN 0-439-68985-6

12 11 10 9 8 7 6 5 4 5 6 7 8 9 10/0

Printed in the U.S.A. 23

First Scholastic printing, January 2005